poetry by
David R. Miller

Photography by
David and Ann Miller

Island Time

Copyright ©2018 by David Miller

ALL RIGHTS RESERVED

For information regarding permission to reproduce parts of this book, write to Bedford House Publications Post Office Box 3184, Topsail Beach NC 28445 or contact us at bedfordhousepub@gmail.com

Miller, David R.
  Island Time

ISBN-13: 978-1727442618 (CreateSpace-Assigned)
ISBN-10: 172744261X
BISAC: Poetry / General

Printed in Charleston SC, USA

Book Design by David and Ann Miller

To Ann
who has given me...

Island Time
(and everything else)

Island Time

The Beach House

Dawning	3
Boundless	4
Island Time	5
South on 17	6
Barrier Islands	7
Stormfront	11
Tantrum	12
The Source	13
Healing	15
The Eye	16
Things That Enchant the Eye	18
Promise	22
Moonrise	23

Transparency

And Here I Am	27
The Cave	28
Manic	30
Blackbird	31
Dirty Laundry	33
Prism	34
Into the White Light	36
Chatterbox	38
Forensic Hypnosis	39
Wordstorm	40
Deathsong	41

Bedford Street	42
Broken	44
Transparency	46
Georgetown	48
Sapare Aude	52
Faith Is...	56
Canaan's Curse	58
Iscariot	59

Love Taps

First Kiss	65
Adoramus	67
Nature	68
Windswept	70
Footprints	74
Reunion	75
Nocturne	76
Connection	79
To the Masters	80
First Frost	81
K626	83
November	84
Fantasy	86
Just Past One	87
I Told You So	92

Woolgathering

Watching Dolphins	97
Fishermen	98
Dot Com	100

Woolgathering	101
A Marital Situation	105
Wednesday Morning	106
Faux Mink	107
The Drawl	108
Poetry 101	109
Creation	112

About the Author 117

The Beach House

Dawning

Wispy cirri bathed in crimson glow
spread across the firmament and wash
the darkness from the world and from the ash
gray dolor.

Majestic color:
expanding reds and yellows, violet hues,
and every shade of blue you can imagine
overwhelm my senses and infuse
my wakening,

broadening
consciousness with sensuality,
the soaring sensuality of one
who stands enthralled in deep serenity,
acceptance, peace.

Resentments cease
as meditation calms the troubled mind;
elation rises as the sun ascends
the loving sky. In this I find
my dawning.

Boundless

The shorebird skims the ripple of the tide –
a blue-grey blur against the morning pale;
sandpipers chase the waves away and delve
coquinas; seagulls scavenge in the shale;
above, a helicopter from Lejeune
and the pale vestige of the waning moon.

What can the feeble spirit comprehend?
I know that God is in each grain of sand,
the scurry-paths of pipers, in the waves,
and in the roiling sea, and far beyond.

Beyond blue skies there is a deeper sky:
our little planet whirls around a star
that whirls around a galaxy that whirls
among ten billion galaxies or more!

Amid this whirling, dizzy roundelay
I sit alone and watch the dolphins play.

Island Time

We've fantasized for years; we've quacked about
a house down by the ocean, talked of it
in dreamy tones – a distant dream, without
substance or definition. We would sit
pretending that the bean field was the sea;
the crows were gulls; the noisy traffic, surf;
the deer were dolphins; pines became palm trees.
We'd spin these wild frivolities and laugh.

But now we've found our home on Topsail Beach –
A townhouse in a rustic, beachy town.
The papers all went through without a hitch;
A week from Tuesday morning, we go down.

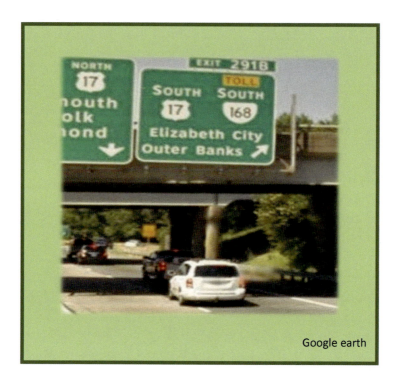

Google earth

South on 17

We braved that claustrophobic Bay Bridge Tunnel;
we fought that traffic through Virginia Beach;
we left Route Sixty-Four just south of Norfolk.
Paradise will soon be in our reach.

Barrier Islands

An indiscernible thread
–as slender as a hair,
as fragile as a reed–
lies upon the map
where the Atlantic coast
bends to crescent:
a barrier between
the Carolina Mainland
and the ferocious storms.

Hurricanes will come
just as they always have
for untold centuries.
But sleep well, Carolina;
your barrier is here
and we will take the brunt.
Our homes confront the sea,
standing defiantly;
shoulder to shoulder, we are
your sturdy paladins,
courageous sentinels.

Stormfront

The deep grey sky is the advancing horde;
Carolina blue is in retreat;
the stiffly brandished reds and blues
foretell the thunderous victory.
Today is indoor day.

Imposter Sun is sleeping in turquoise;
the glistening man has ridden by six times.
The South Wind tries to turn the pages.
The empty chalice has gone cold;
the vision's out of focus.

The angels call to me in many voices;
half my face is hot, one eye is blind.
The creature leads the helpless child,
the sisters marching south in step –
the wind blows against them.

A young boy stands to face the hurricane;
the lone man struggles with a heavy load.
The soldier stops to find his way.
I hear the women chattering
but can't make out their words.

Tantrum

The ocean, with its mystery and power,
yesterday was glassy as a pond,
its gentle ripples lapping on the sand.
Today its heaving threatens to devour
the dunes, to wash the beach away,
as though Poseidon were a petulant child
enraged because he cannot get his way.

The Source

Spellbound, I behold the source
of light and life. The Universe

beckons my body's energy
to join its oneness and be free

from isolation, to align
my being with the Tao and find
its peace.

                The phases of the moon,
the swirling galaxies, the sun,

the curvature of time and space
carry my spirit to the place

where I am one with the creator;
I am part of something greater

than myself. Infinities
of nature's wonders pass through me.

But what are all these musings worth?
The practicalities of earth

confine me to this workaday
existence. Frenzied disarray

and chaos vex my troubled mind.
I know I must dispel this kind
of temporal disconnect and find

        my center.

A slow, deep breath; a calming sigh
silences the din of my

frenetic thinking. Only then,
these meditations once again

will meld me with the primal source
of light and life: the Universe.

Healing

It seems that sanity has settled in,
or something that resembles sanity.
I've gained emotional stability,
and time is taming that incessant din,
the omnipresent dart-sparks in my brain.

Time, that is, and my trusty medicine –
psychotic medications, time, and prayer.

Time, meds, prayer, and a home by the sea,
where dolphins play and seagulls call to me,
and where the sea-breeze whispers in my ear.

I watch coquinas magically appear
and disappear again with each new wave;
in seashell-quest I walk along the strand,
and watch the shorebirds scurry on the sand,
and a ghost crab digs his not-so-secret cave.

> So, is this sanity, lucidity,
> or just a pleasanter insanity?

The Eye

The stratus shroud is darkly omnipresent;
the slate grey sky's so dark it's almost black –
so ominous and threatening. I can't
imagine how the rain is holding back!

It seems there'd be no daylight in between
this blackish cloud and inky black of space,
but as I sit alone and watch this scene
a stratospheric wind insinuates

and rips apart the curtain to expose
a sun-touched cotton cumulus behind
in contrast nearly blinding. There it is,
as bright and silver as a brand new dime.

And now that ovoid gap of burnished white
is further parted, and a dab of blue
reveals itself; the darkness cedes to light;
tomorrow's promised sunshine pierces through.

Sitting on my deck this stormy day,
I'm witness to a miracle! I see
the azure blue, through silver white, through grey;
the eye of God is looking down at me.

Things That Enchant the Eye

The clouds that cushion the falling sun
exploding in orange and crimson,

the shadows creeping across the dunes,
the dolphin that plays in the ocean,

the tourist that leaves a crust of bread
and tosses it up to the seagull,

the piper that chases the waves away,
the herons, so supple and graceful:

these are the things that enchant the eye
of poet, of child, of seeker;

these are the things that I want to share
with you, my wife, my lover.

Promise

Emblazoned ribbons halfway up the sky
soaring to a lofty precipice
from the olive gray horizon. High
above our rain-drenched little town, it is
the promise washed in colorful array.
I shared a rainbow with my love today.

Moonrise

I've seen the sun rise often, but seldom the moon;
so when the full, unclouded moon last night
rose up from out the ocean's full horizon
in pock-marked powder-pinkish through the haze,
and slowly dribbled color on the waves,
and while behind, that other crimson light
deferred to cede the heavens for the night
to the understudy, I, in awe,
stood on the sand between them, very small,
most likely imperceptible to these,
the weekend tourists in from who-knows-where,
preoccupied and gussied for the night,
who watch it from their hotel balconies.

And Here I Am

I have had an epiphany!
When William Butler Yeats
was born he had a deformed Siamese Twin.

The Dublin doctor looked at them
and gravely shook his head,
and as per nineteenth-century medicine,

decided that the sickly little
runt, the lesser one,
was less than human, should be cut away

and left to die. But when the parson
heard of this, he called
the folk of Sandymount to come and pray.

The parish came together and
their fervent prayers went out
for that pathetic excuse for a human.

And God, in his great mercy and
his omnipresent wisdom,
decided this sick soul should live again.

The Cave

> *Think you of the fact that a deaf person*
> *cannot hear. Then, what deafness may we*
> *not all possess? What senses do we lack*
> *that we cannot see and cannot hear*
> *another world all around us?*
> —Frank Herbert

Down in the cave Plato imagined,
    shackled to the wall
with head and eyes immobilized,
    I watch the shadows flit

and dart across the span of my
    reality, and fall
so silently away. I savor
    momentary bits

of sensory experience:
    the dampness of the air,
the tickle as a drop
    of perspiration trails along

my cheek, the wafting odor of
    the stagnant pools, the rare
and fleeting glimpse of mouse or bat.
    I sense the evensong

of waning light and of the fading

      shadows as my world
descends into its cycle of impending
      darkness. Beams

of dusty light slant inward, and
      the crimson specters hurled
upon my wall excite the terror
      of forbidden dreams.

In dreams my weak, atrophied limbs,
      of their own accord,
transport me to a mystic realm
      of free and open space

where shadows take on substance, and
      my new-found life affords
unfathomed freedom!

                But, I know
that there is no such place.

Manic

The visions of night have all wasted away;
I've opened my eyes to a vagabond day:
maniacal soul, despised by the light–
> *a martyr in solitude, crying for night.*

The artist beside me, creating at will –
so little she knows of the visions she'll fill
when I have retreated to empty delight–
> *a martyr in solitude, crying for night.*

The hare to the trap and the moth to the flame,
again and again it will turn out the same,
try as I will, with all of my might–
> *a martyr in solitude, crying for night.*

In scraping the dregs of my life's only dream,
pathetically cringing from terrors unseen,
and sucking the life from the waning starlight–
> *a martyr in solitude, crying for night.*

Blackbird
(allegro ma non troppo)

There is a blackbird set among
the heaven sent and tightly strung
harps of hell fire torment can you
tell that I've been thinking? [Bingo!]
hey a heckler! whaddya know
and I am seeking savor flavor
saver favor well eight-to-
the-bar it seems but never eight
odd numbers always work out better
monometer trimeter
better still pentameter
better and better than ever heptameter
[except this ain't no nothin'-meter]
Accentual? [Accentual!]
diffracted broken promises
and sunburn on my coconut
Delphic Oracle [say what?!]
that's Yeats you ass don't interrupt
fifth foot a spondee cause iamb
[amb not!] but maybe this there all
the golden codgers [Fal-de-ral!]
a stream of consciousness the five-
line stanza sit alone and pray
and nine-eleven seems to never
happen [split infinitive]
and never end a sentence line
or phrase a preposition with

leave her [leave her?] Beaver Cleaver
[take a cleaver to the beaver!]
hush I said what say another
page awaits you as you drone
to men who sink and rise [and sink]
and rise [and sink again you say]
the blackbirds still ensemble cool
and bright and coffee's almost done
the object of my secret love
[so inappropriate!] so pull
and push a little if you like
to boldly go [oops there it is]
it seems to go unnoticed [   ]

Dirty Laundry

Is there a word
for the shade of green

where, after the long night's
brutal storms,

the wet leaves in the foreground
glow with reptile iridescence,

thinly veiling
the dark, shadowy woods,

as the sun insinuates
into the narrow, well-defined space

between the blue-red-yellow
dawning horizon

and the clouds' dark truth?

Prism

The prism yields diffracted, broken
      promises of glory.
I failed to sense deception; still
      I fail to sense belief.

The lying masses failed me; scarred
      and scorned, I seek relief
in rooms of seething silence. It's
      that never-ending story.

Dependence on that poison nearly
      cost my sanity,
roiling through my body
      and infusing every cell.

I know too well the shame and pain
      of sweating, tremulous hell;
I know too well the sorrow of
      the broken family.

Tiny darts of lightning in
      the corner of my eye
vanish as I turn to see.
      Hot lava surges through

my veins; I'm sweating through my clothes
      and everything I do
goes wrong, so wrong. The simple patterns

      undulate awry.

Seclusion is a poor lost harvest
      rotting in the fields.
Fly-infested loneliness
      rotting in my brain

and ringing loudly in my ears;
      sanity I feign.
And broken promises of glory
      the broken prism yields.

Into the White Light

Late last night I walked a dark,
      secluded country road;
a rolling, dewy pasture spread
      before me and I slowed
beside a clean, white fence that etched
      the contour of the hills.
The undulating hills were like
      the furrows of the sea
and each hill was the grazing place
      for some variety
           of farm animal.

Upon those little hills some cows
      and sheep serenely grazed
beneath the nineteenth crescent of
      the moon. I was amazed
to see that on one of the hills
      five chewing horses stood;
shoulder-to-shoulder, tail-to-tail,
      the five stood in a row;
and on another hill five goats
      ate clover in the glow
           of the waning moon.

Similarly, there were five
      of every animal;
five-by-five, each kind to kind,
      each on its little hill;

    these quintets crooned their creature noises,
        all in unison;
    five cows lowed synchronously;
        five sheep bleated together.
    All told, there were hundreds in
        that finely blended choir.
            They behaved as one.

    If one goat bent to nibble on some grass,
        the five bent down;
    if one horse swept his tail to shoo a fly,
        five tails swept round.
    Above this pastoral song and dance
        an aurora then appeared
    and brightened with the din's crescendo
        to a blinding light!
    I felt my body being carried
        off into the night,
            and I woke in tears.

Chatterbox

Eighteen blossoms
of glossy plastic
dispense the nectar we boiled, sugared, and iced;
we pipe-cleaned and baby-bottle-brushed
the red petals and glass bulbs,
helping nature along.

Still, they quarrel:
the Rubies buzz the Plain Jane Grays,
the Coppers dive-bomb the Mottled Browns,
indignantly, greedily,
they lobster up
and chatter like frenzied monkeys
as if it were a zero-sum game,
as if his would diminish hers,
as if there were not abundance,
as if we would stop providing.

> *My friend visited yesterday.*
> *She slathers over punctuation*
> *as if conversation were a zero-sum game,*
> *as if yours might diminish hers,*
> *as if the room might run out of words.*

Forensic Hypnosis
For Heather

Her memories of childhood are not bright;
her childhood lasted longer that it should.
She said they're mostly repressed anyway.
I said if she were hypnotized, she might
regress, restore them.

                      "Even if I could,"
she said, "no thanks! Just keep them locked away!
The memories my subconscious mind has blocked
must be block-worthy ones. And thus my brain
protects me and preserves my sanity
(such as it is). So no, I won't unlock
the steely cage that bars those monsters in.
My blessed ignorance ensconces me.

I only wish some memories I've made
as an adult would similarly fade."

Wordstorm

Wordstorm faltering
parroting, pandering,
aimless meanderings
caught in the swirling
of spritely devils'
dusty drivel

        richstream – negative
        whiteshot – unalive
        false reality
        trite banality
        blathering outpour
        linedog failure

                elocutions
                half-stiche divisions
                trivia festers
                infinite blunders
                clumsy accentuals
                nothing original

Deathsong

The peepholes in my skull
afford a limited view.
Ahead: ten thousand opaque, finite things.
Behind: black-blind and vulnerable.

Dartsparks,
in a globe of bone
are strapped to a fleshy toy,
a broken device,
until it slows, stops, cools,
until it is cloaked, burned, buried;

light,
so long bushelled and ill-defined
blossoms to Panorama,
tethered to no dogma,
unfatigued and unbounded,
aligned,
absorbed into One.

Bedford Street

1. I Think I Would
A solitary bird,
with no mate or flock,
skips at the level of treetops.

I'll never know
what lures him here or there,
but I wonder that he,
blessed with the ability,
wouldn't fly much higher.

2. Avant-garde
One – perhaps a gander (though I doubt it) –
banked and took a different course, alone,
staking out another way,
disconnected from the flying "V."

It could be she was searching for her mate –
her soul mate, lost to predator or gun –
or perhaps she was aware
instinctively there would be water there.

The others of the flock become confused;
the graceful "V" became an awkward "U,"
a crooked, asymmetric arc,
a funny, twisted sort of question mark.

The flock banked to the left and followed her,

caught up, regrouped to their familiar form,
symbiotically joined.
And she, of course, was flying at the point.

3. Requiem Aeternam
The orbs and tablets, crosses, monoliths,
some in place a hundred years or more
and rendered unintelligible by
a century of wind and rain. Before
you pass by, stop and look. Consider them;
by their stones' grandeur, some were very rich –
sea captains, merchants or judges perhaps.
Most were poor, yet they, too, held a niche
in our community. Look at them now,
the haughty, the down-trodden—no difference—
rotting in a weedy churchyard, surrounded
 by a creaky, black and rusted wrought iron fence.

4. Trash Truck
As I walk the misty dawn,
my peaceful reverie
is rudely interrupted,
assaulted
by its sudden passing—
the sharp hiss of air brakes,
the doppled-down rumble,
the thick, hot burst
of garbage-scented wake

Broken

I.
As I sat reading
in that old
recliner
that has shaped itself
so comfortably
to my languor,
dozing in Bach's
lilting air,
I was startled
by a thump
on the storm door.
Out on the step,
a small heap
of iridescent
green sank into death.
The Greenback
hummingbird
hadn't seen
the glass. As I
picked it up,
its lifeless eyes
stared into
nothingness;
its head lolled
awkwardly
from its broken neck.

II.
Across the road
a shredded
blue tarpaulin
shrouds the old boat;
the bungees wind-slap
her algae-
jaded hull,
her trailer's
fenders bent
and rusted through;
the cinder block
buttress prop
toppled long ago.

My lonely neighbor,
broken of spirit,
grief-etched and
weather-worn,
scythes the weeds around
the dry-rot
flattened tires,
remembering
(I might suppose)
the sun-tanned
children laughing
and swimming,
and skiing
in her wake.

Transparency

Spring

    The seashell's placed
    among the things I love,
    concentric swirls
    of pink and creamy white
    converging
    magic-rationally;
    the tapered end
    a hollow arrowhead.

    You chose that shell
    for me among all those
    given to you
    by God that afternoon.
    It's delicate as lace
    and fragile as my soul:
    empty, dead as stone.

Summer

    Angry sun descends
    into the gathering
    black horizon;
    shimmering devils
    rise up from the street,
    hot black tar
    clings to my feet.

Autumn
>Clouds gust in
>on thick autumn.
>Pedestrians
>turn collars
>to the chill:
>Brown leaves whirl
>their tribal dance.

Winter
>Cherry blossoms.
>Petals on
>the sidewalk,
>drenched by rain
>and trodden
>black and ugly
>by a thousand
>footsteps.
>
>With eyes downcast
>I've walked this way,
>again and again,
>day after day.
>
>I never saw the blossoms
>when they were on the tree.
>Now the branches all are bare;
>I've missed the opportunity.

Georgetown

Once,
in an easy time,
    so I am told,
that stately house
across the road
stood two miles
to the south,
in the middle
of the town
on stately
North Bedford Street,
next to the church
with the stately
white steeple,
across from the stately
funeral home.

There,
in an innocent time
    so I am told,
it was the local
Youth Center,
the hangout where
the clumsy adolescents
danced to vinyl 45's,
played checkers and cards
with checkers and cards,
ping-pong with paddles

not joysticks,
and their text messages
were stealthily passed
on paper folded
into origami.

Then,
in a restless time,
    so I am told,
the house was jacked-up,
trailered, and
hauled out here,
and became
the stately office
for a local CPA.
Where the
clumsy adolescents
once gathered and danced,
the clumsy grownups
now budget their budgets
and cheat on their taxes
and fill out their forms.

    (Budgets
        and taxes
           and forms
                ..... oh my!)

It is Sunday now
and the house

is still, like
the faded flags in front
are limp and still:
the faded
Delaware Diamond
and the faded
Stars-n-Stripes,
drooped
in the still and steamy
summer
morning.

Now,
in this stagnant time,
    so I am told
where that house once stood,
there is a park
strewn with trash
where the Friends of Bill gather
before the noon
AA meeting
in the church's
musty basement.

In the dull shadow
of the algae-green steeple,
they all sit
on the swings
and picnic tables;
they smoke and talk

about who has relapsed,
who is screwing who,
who cut their ankle bracelet off,
and who has gone to jail;

and sweaty white women
sag the benches

> *" 'cuz the walk to Waw-mart is
> pert'near a mile an' I gotta have a
> cig'rette and ketch my breath, an'
> how come don't no damn buses
> come out here anyways?"*

and the Mexican kids play soccer
and laugh
all day long.

Sapare Aude[1]

> Article I, Section 1: All legislative Powers herein granted shall be **vested** in a Congress of the United States, which shall consist of a Senate and House of Representatives.

Veritas Omnia Vincit[2]

I.
And when will all this shit begin to change?
How will it change, or should it change, and should
some stupid, privileged fraternity
thrust us on to this destructive course?

Over what, as individuals,
and over what, collectively, do we
have control? Or should we have? And should
we ask then, "what is just?" or, "what just is?"

But are we now so arrogant that we,
the uncontrolled, entitled, cannot see
before us now the slow and crumbling end
of what was once an inspiration? And

---

[1] Dare to know
[2] Truth conquers all

the most important question we can ask,
the most significant issue of the day
is not, "Dear God, where do we go from here?"
but, "Where's the camera? Who is there to blame?"

II.
Remembering the old days when
      I used to have a cause,
I know now I was in this just because...
      ...well, just because.

If your persona is defined
      by adamant belief
what happens when you've lost your faith?
      So now I know the grief

of youthful idealism gone awry,
and I don't even question why.

The daffodils are in full bloom;
      the grass is radiant green;
the war is half a world away,
      not felt, not heard, not seen,

not even thought about by selfish
      people here at home;

the price of gasoline
      is more important.

This sick game we play!

It's ignorance; it's arrogance;
And nothing makes a difference.

A baby in a car seat with
      a plastic steering wheel
thinks he's really driving, and
      I know just how he feels.

I believed we made a difference,
      too – all those protests,
debates, and arguments – so who
      the hell did we impress!?

And now the cause is lost, our hearts are bruised,
and I regret the way that I was used.

III.
Dogmatic viciousness is at the heart
of faceless carnage.
      He is the terrorist!

May his writhing soul be torn apart
and cast headlong into the deep abyss!

Apocalyptic musings long have called
the stupid, shallow-minded hordes to war.

The salivating masses are enthralled;
the newborn fawn dismembered by the boar.

The wanderings of Abram's seed shall end
when from the cloud the promised one breaks forth

in cataclysmic majesty, descends,
and moves his hand in judgment of the earth.

Quando coeli movendi sunt et terra³
blood shall be spilled amid the great tumult.

Ruin shall be to all the sons of Sarah,
the ignorant proclaiming, "Deus vult!"⁴

---

³When heaven and earth move
⁴God proclaims it

Faith is...
(April 16, 1178 BC)

The tribesmen saw the devil eat the sun;
bit by greedy bit it was devoured,
and midday turned to night. They cringed in fear,
terrorized by this malicious power.

The world turned dark and cold. The awful beast,
unsated, turned its gaze to humankind,
its round, black face ablaze with fires of hell!
All those who dared to watch were smitten blind!

The wise one said, "we must implore the gods!"
The elders desperately chanted prayer;
the women beat the drums; the warriors rose
and flailed the sacred dance around the fire.

The gods responded; they took up the battle
and slayed the demon, and the sun was freed.

> They chanted and they danced; the sun returned.
> And that was all the proof they'd ever need.

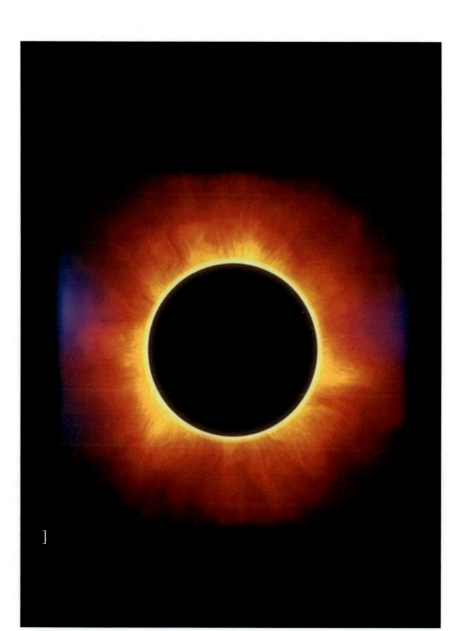

Canaan's Curse
(Genesis 9:20)

Disgusting sot, naked on the floor!
His beard is caked with puke; he's ashen grey.
His days of building ships are long since gone –
no doubt the animals would turn away.

He gradually shakes his black-out fog.
Who brought this blanket, who was it that tried
to cover up his shame? He doesn't care;
his head is splitting and his mouth is dry.

Oh God! He realizes, he's been raped!
It wasn't some unspeakable nightmare.
Violated while half comatose!
He knows it, all the tell-tale signs are there.

And piecing all the memories together
of this licentious, vile atrocity,
he realizes it was Ham, his son
who had committed this debauchery!

It doesn't bode well for humanity
that this sick man and his accursed brood –
detestable, incestuous – would be
the only ones worth saving from the flood.

Iscariot
(Matthew 27: 1-10)

I.
Twenty-nine coins of "*precious*" silver,
thrown to the floor; grovel if you want.

The thirtieth I used to buy this rope.
And now here I stand beneath this tree,

this heavy branch; I step up on this stool,
wondering how it ever came to this.

I am Iscariot.
    This is my story.

II.
When the Master called, I dropped my nets
and walked away; I gladly followed him.

For these three years I have been called Apostle;
I have been his faithful proselyte.

"I will give up everything I have,
make whatever sacrifice you ask."

That is what I told him.
    Little did I know.

So just imagine my bewilderment,

my shock, despair, when he pulled me aside

to tell me how his plan was to unfold,
and how his ministry would culminate.

To maximize his impact on the world,
for ancient prophesies to be fulfilled,

there had to be a martyr. He himself
must suffer execution, crucifixion,

and there would be a role
    that I would have to play.

III.
Peter was his favorite I think.
    Stupid Peter!

He always seemed to put his foot in his mouth.
The coward! Last night when the chips were down

he bellowed out, "I am not one of them.
I swear I do not even know the man!"

    (cock-a-doodle-doo....)

He'd been called Simon; Jesus changed his name.
"Upon this Rock I'll build my church." He said.

Some rock he is!

> Some sturdy rock!

I'm told my brethren, Matthew, Luke, and John
have already begun to draft their gospels.

And why is it that Mark was singled out
and given secrets no one else could know?

Oh, how he smirked!
            And Philip, James, or Thomas –
was I not as faithful as them all?

In his eyes,
    evidently not...

IV.
So I was made to connive with the Romans –
Pilate and all of his despicable minions –

and to accept that bag of bloody money
(Silver??) as if that somehow might appease.

When I kissed his cheek, I whispered, "Rabbi,
tell me why it has to be this way."

He didn't answer, but said for all to hear,
"Why must you betray me with a kiss?"

BECAUSE YOU TOLD ME TO,
    THAT'S WHY!!

V.
And now, my name will live in infamy,
eternally synonymous with evil:

Judas the betrayer – Judas, traitor!
It was not supposed to end like this.

So I will toss my rope over the branch,
and wear the noose, and kick away the stool.

Lord, I know of your great sacrifice.

Well, this is mine.
    I hope it is eno-

Love Taps

First Kiss

We walked beneath October stars
and fingernail crescent,
walking,
not as one with a place to go,
a thing to do, or business to conduct –
walking,
not for transport
or conveyance – points A to B.

We lingered at each step,
savoring the firsts of everything:
first time each-to-each revealing secrets,
first time arm-in-arm or hand-in-hand,
we tacitly consider possibilities.

Where will this slow walk take us?
As I contemplate the brevity,
of this time together
and a future far too brief,
is it right to waste a single day,
or let a silent second pass?

Such thoughts stir my consciousness;
I let them linger for a moment
then pass, without judgment.
Inhaling deeply,
absorbing the cypress redolence
and last of the honeysuckle,

enjoying the depth
of the very breath itself –
breath
for breath's own sake,
I realize with tinges of regret
that we have reached her house
and that good-night has come.

I pause to hinder
the progress of
goodbye;

I pause to commit
this moment
to future
reminiscence.

Adoramus

I'll grip the magic feather in my hand
and leap from that high precipice above
the rocky crag; I'll soar upon the wind,
and at the thought of you my soul will rise
and breathlessly ascend the infinite skies.

Nature
for Ann

The sun, its searing, scorching heat
traversing vast reaches of space
and filtered through the miles-deep atmosphere,
still bakes the sand beneath my feet
and burns the skin on my back and face
and blinds my eyes with its oppressive glare.

The ocean with its churning tide,
tempestuous and merciless,
unleashes the tsunami's murderous hell
and tosses mighty ships aside
like broken toys upon the crests
and valleys of its heaving, roguish swell.

The Earth, seething, teetering
in balance, fiercely grinds and quakes.
Volcanoes gushing from its molten core
throb and spasm. All-consuming
wildfires, born of lightning strikes
and dry-wind-driven, feed my primal fear.

> *My love for you — my passion-drowned*
> *and joy-filled spirit, heart, and mind—*
> *exhilarates my life like rolling thunder,*
> *bellows like the mighty sound*
> *of pounding surf and howling wind*
> *and burns within me hotter than the sun.*

Windswept

I.
I've changed this house;
I feel it in my bones;
the deer are my guests;
my eyes are swollen shut.

Kiss me home...

        home...

Sparkle me,
     eyes of my daughter,
bring music home,
     my son.

The pluck of the strings,
enticement of sound,
the young man sings
and the world spins around.

Sleepless,
in the creak of night,
My brain is called

     ... Legion!

I am engulfed in longing;

It was to be our first kiss,
long and slow and sweet.
Instead she turned her head away
and offered me her cheek.

II.
Groaning in the day's long labor,
he glared from far away,
from the burnished agony,
     once...
          long ago.

   (I know
   God isn't dead,
   but he seems
   to be sleeping
   this year.)

Who is the lost musician?
Who is the silent angel?
Who is the brave officer?

Patience, for an hour, my love...

III.
I have changed my shirt;
I have feared the blue sign;
I have kicked the door;
I have gazed into seasons;
I have been sung to dying;

I have been sung to life.
I have pressed my face to the glass;
I have known desperation.
I have cried to the crystal soldiers;
I have screamed for the Dark Man.
I have been the troll;
I have hidden beneath the bridge,
I have puked on tracks.
I have crawled into broken places;
I have cut my hands;
I have shaken beyond control;
I have guzzled the poison;
I have known the long, deep breath of solitude;
I have felt the hum of isolation;
I have swallowed the darkness;
I have been swallowed by the darkness,
I have....
        I have,

the darkness....

IV.
But will I see the God-swept shimmer?
Will it shimmer over all things,
    or just the sea?

Is the shadow less than light?
Does the rabbit's gaze accuse me?
Do the stars dance with the moon?
Do the sun's bright feathers

      darken me to iron?

Don't follow me,
Sweet one...

Let the children come to me;
suffer them not.

Let the siren-song touch my lips
and let the angels waltz in my arms.

God sings to me;
the bright sky calls to me;
the child whispers to me;
the river cares for me;
the ocean sighs for me
      in the tide's dark loftiness,

I am sleepless again...

      sleepless again...

...again.

Footprints

Walking through the streets in the moon's soft glow,
the quiet sweep of snowy night befall,
I leave my tired footprints in the snow.

I know the pain of loneliness; I know
my loneliness, my bitterness, my gall.
Walking through the streets in the moon's soft glow.

The wind makes wispy devils as I go;
the earth is shrouded in a pure white pall;
I leave my tired footprints in the snow.

The clouds reveal the pallid moon, and shadows
appear and fade upon the road and wall
as I walk through the streets in the moon's soft glow.

I am so tired; my step's unstable, slow;
and slowly trudging, careful not to fall,
I leave my tired footprints in the snow.

I've walked for miles with many more to go –
my loneliness the snowy shroud I draw.
Walking through the streets in the moon's soft glow,
I leave my tired footprints in the snow.

Reunion

We were friends,
how long ago?

At the bookstore yesterday
I did not recognize you.

      (Forgive me)

You have changed.
I was curious;

I wondered
what had happened.

      (I was too polite to ask.)

Nocturne

The darkness of our room and of our minds
serves only to conceal contempt we wind
around each other in the light of day
when trifling vexations all emerge.
And when night comes again we cast away
indifference, succumb to wanton sway,
surrendering to our desire's upsurge.

In trying to recapture first impressions,
we're riding on the tide of shifting passions;
we are entangled in the afterglow
of breathless ardor that will not suffice
to justify our ill-bred quid pro quo.
We've come round once again to new hello
between the inescapable goodbyes.

Connection

In the old hotel across the street,
    a single window glows,
and I suppose that someone is
    awake, as I'm awake
at four o'clock, before the dawn,
    that someone else's brain
is reeling, turning churning some
    unwelcomed cognizance
of rueful memories; perhaps
    they're scribbling in their own
pathetic dog-eared journal useless
    scribble-gibberish.

The eastern sky is glowing now
    and Venus ushers in
the rising sun, and in that glow
    I hear the lonely surf
and raucous crickets on the dune.
    The only evidence
that life exists: the crickets, the glowing
    window there, and I.

To the Masters

You seem to notice everything you see
and not a single sound goes undetected:
wind chimes in the distance, rainbows in
the black and oily puddles, testy birds
squawking on the limb.
>*Azaleas afire in white and red.*

Phrases bend, compliant to your will;
you effortlessly spin a metaphor;
images seem to leap out from the page;
the reader feels the pain and shares the joy
the artist's pen conveys,
>*Azaleas afire in white and red.*

The thought-provoking allegory and
the wispy pangs of memory are to you
obedient subordinates. I've been
endowed with just the modest talent to
appreciate your genius.
>*Azaleas afire in white and red.*

As I aspire to take the art I love
up to the highest level I can muster
I look for inspiration to the masters.
Euterpe doles the gift as she sees fit.
>*Azaleas afire in white and red.*

First Frost

This morning kids etch initials
                in the frost

that's formed on cars' hoods and laugh
                with steamy breath.

Into the first frost of fall
                I step outside

and feel the cold air assault
                my face and arms.

A year has gone by and cycles
                round again;

summer wanes, cowering to
                the autumn's chill.

I shiver, not with the cold,
                but with the fear

of growing old. Autumn makes
                me realize

that as each day passes, winter
                closes in.

no matter how I deny it,

        death is real.

I watch the town as it stirs
                and comes to life;

I watch the sun inch its way
                into the dawn;

I watch the moon sink into
                a stand of trees;

I turn and go back into
                the house, alone.

K626

Pendulous silence
(scattered coughs)
unresolved dissonance
the frenzy
of Confutatis
dominant seventh lingers
in reverberation
strings poised
pinky-
        plucked
                pitches
define D-minor
fingers ache for vibrato
bows edgy for downstroke
of twelve-eight cantabile.
From rhythmic breath
and baton's ictus,

Lacrymosa

November

Blessings – fragile blessings –
heaven-sent and tightly-strung,
and with an ill-placed word could tumble down.
              (Pathetic clown!)
The dead and thorny vines are coiled
              into a wreath and hung
      upon an old man's door, unwelcoming.

A harp sings far away
and spongy fog hangs in the air;
space is past – desiderata lost.
              (Albatross!)
The broken speech of light has left
              the angels unaware
      of soft meanderings and orchid days.

The sensitivities
of broken children cry out loud –
the howling of the she-wolf to the moon.
              (It's much too soon!)
From underneath the bridge the troll
              with bloodshot eyes slinks out;
      the yellow leaves are falling from the trees.

Can you hear, soft birds
on solid limbs, the broken stones?
The shimmer lies beyond the woman's sight.
              (the blinding light!)

She cannot hear the desperate calling
    of the fragile bones
  or sense the moon or understand its words.

Like crickets spirits come;
no fish are swimming in the stream;
the moon is flimsy as a fingernail.
    (Doomed to fail!)
I have a penchant; I allow it
     to invade my dream.
  I wander in the forest, dropping crumbs.

Fantasy

Whenever fantasy's encountered
so, to stay my evil soul
when in blood my deed's misgiven,
there I milk my ravaged fold

for nothing. To feel your arms surround me
as to the branch the vine shall cling,
I will abide your reminiscent
rhyme. Do you wish that I should sing

to our encountered night's remembrance?
Then, to night's misfortune, be
unto my eyes, your precious beauty
lain unto sad hearts to see.

Just Past One

Where the heavy
 rain and wind
April-long
and dark-cloud-high
glisten the road
this day new winds
began to blow
and just past one
and forever
my heart soars
forth and above
into the
crystal blue...
this evening
one marched
her words and mine
      moved
         slowly
      down
and afterward
I looked behind
where she
and my heart tread
I watched
long after
she had gone
        goodnight
here her words

remain
tomorrow
her words
will return
again to me
patiently
where nothing moves
beyond the blue
and bluest-of-blue
and where
nothing moves
but arrows
flashing wildly
there I wait
she of unknown
voice
and name
will return
again to me...

I Told You So

Life, the stubborn lady,
struggled to hold me
as I struggled to break away—
lured by the Temptress Death,
I settled into darkness.

But tenacious Life had other plans.
When she dragged me back
I screamed and cursed;
angry and frustrated,
I had failed in my last pursuit,
lost the only control I had left.

~~~~~

    Now, she winks at me in the sun,
    smiles in the summer sky—
    my wife's kiss is her kiss;
    my grandchild's laughter is her laughter—
    she nudges me
    with love-taps of cool rain,
    whispers in the softness of the breeze,

        "see, see... I told you so!"

Woolgathering

They're Just For Watching the Dolphins.   Honest!

The wheel? The car? The microwave?
    I'm 'fraid I must dispute.
Mankind's greatest invention is
    the two-piece bathing suit.

No, I am <u>*NOT*</u> a dirty old man;
    I'd say I'm all the norm.
But I guess binoculars at the beach
    would be bad form!

Fishermen

Every day the fishermen fish;
      fishing is what they do.
They cast their lines into the surf
      and crack another brew.
With their coolers filled with Buds
they float to heaven on the suds.

Their planted rods are like a forest
      we must negotiate;
kids can't swim or play within
      the space they dominate,
and if you're close you're bound to hear
words unfit for little ears.

Sometimes as we stroll the strand
      chatting, with our minds
occupied with other things,
      we'll walk into their lines.
If it had been steel wire instead
it may have severed off my head!

I've seen so many fishermen
      along this beachy scene.
Despite their histrionics there's
      one thing I've never seen:
For all their ostentatious kitsch,
I've never seen one catch a fish.

Dot Com

> *"lookin' fer love in all the wrong places"*
> —*Johnny Lee*

If all who claimed to love to walk the beach
    walked the beach,
you couldn't move around for all those walkers.

If everyone who claimed to love to dance
    danced,
the world would rumble with their dancing.

    "I love to listen to all kinds of music."
        (If it's on MTV!)
    "I love to read the great philosophers."
        (Or People Magazine!)
    "I love to go explore exotic places."
        (The KOA trailer camp!)
    "I love to try the gourmet restaurants."
        (If I pick up the tab!)

The ones who want no drama could win Tony's!
Her ex-boyfriend is looking for a fight!
Her pictures must be ten years old at least.
And baggage? Hell, she carries Samsonite!

        (But then again, she didn't get
        much of a prize either, did she?)

Woolgathering

On my Calendar app I clicked

and a dialog box appeared:

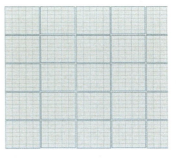

For fun I clicked to view one hundred years.

Thirty six thousand,
five hundred
and twenty five days
popped up,
all in little boxes,
all shrunk to fit the screen;
it resembled course blue fabric,
a tightly woven wool.

And it occurred to me

that somewhere on that screen
is the day of my death;
on one of those little boxes
the wool would be rent between
my life and death existences.

Ah yes, but which one is it?
Which of those stitches will tear?
Which of those tight threads
will jam the loom?

From that torn rag
A few more loose threads will hang,
frazzled and frayed;

these are days of inconvenience
and uncertainty,

rescheduled appointments

and hasty travel plans,

when the minister ministers
the dearly-beloveds,

and the organist practices
What a Friend,

and the church ladies
plan the covered-dish,

and the next-of's go
uptown to meet
the oh so gentle man

in the finely tailored
suit of charcoal gray,

with soft and sad,
and sympathetic eyes,

the voice

> *so soothing,*
>   *so warm,*
>   *and so compassionate,*

Then they'll learn why
the nicest house in town
is the nicest house in town.

Because, behind those soft and sad,
and sympathetic eyes:

"ka-ching, ka-ching! Like fish in a barrel"

And another quality
solid mahogany,

Chestnut Creek,
trendy and sleek,
gold-trimmed,
silk-lined

Worm~Shield® Deluxe

just twenty-seven-thousand-
nine-ninety-nine
ninety-nine*

(financing available to well-qualified mourners)

* plus tax title delivery set-up dealer prep environmental impact assessment fee and other optional equipment not valid is all states offer not valid with any other coupons or promotions prices subject to change without notice actual equipment may vary from illustration crypt pillow flowers and labor charges not included see authorized Worm~Shield® dealer for complete details.

A Marital Situation
painted from memory

Once again, my love, my dear,
you've gone away and left me here

and taken both our sets of keys.
Now you're as free as the summer breeze

but I am stuck; I have no way
to make it through my hectic day.

Please check the hook upon the wall,
your purse, your pockets, check them all

and do me this one favor, please –
leave me, please, one set of keys!

Wednesday Morning
(a view from the deck)

I.
A trio of young ladies jogging by.
I glance up; they are now a group of two
loitering beside the Porta-Potty
(the only derogation of our view).
I didn't see what happened to the third,
but I could take an educated guess.
(Now I don't want to write the only word
that I can think of that would rhyme with "third"
and be applicable to our discussion
of Porta-Potties! Pardon my digression.)

II.
Now that I'm supposed to be a writer
I feel I ought to make a show of writing;
I've suddenly become a pencil-biter
with furrowed brow, absorbed in profound thinking.

These passersby, what if they only knew
that I, the cultivated literati
was working on the third revision to
a poem all about a Porta-Potty?

Faux Mink
(A True Story)

    At a local furniture store, they offer these delightfully cheap and tacky, white, "faux mink" pillows.

    Today I saw a compassionate, conscientious, and obviously **BRILLIANT** young lady[5] approach the manager, quite indignantly, demanding to know if these faux (which she pronounced, FAWKS) mink pillows are made with real fur.

    Right, Princess, they killed a whole herd of fauxes just to make those twenty-five dollar pillows!

    Yes, boys and girls, the "fawk-mink" may be an endangered species, but evidently the "fawk-head" is not.

---

[5] So as not to pander to stereotypical biases, I will NOT mention the young lady's hair color!

The Drawl

~ or ~

*Avoiding Unintentional Disrespect
Derived from Colorful, Colloquial Speech*

In conversation, when I speak of God,
I say that <u>He</u> does this or <u>He</u> does that –
male pronouns simply for convenience,
because it really makes no difference,
and folks won't look at me as if I'm odd
(can't say I'm *not* with any confidence.)

But once I spoke of God as, "*He / She / It,*"
above such trivialities as gender,
because the Power Greater than myself
transcends such mortal trappings. But remember
though, that though God isn't physical,
but purely spiritual, ethereal,
that *"He / She / It"* can garble in the mouth
(especially since we're living in the South!)

Poetry and Poetics 101
(Variations on a theme)

1. Haiku
Roses are reddish
Violets are bluish. Sometimes
I wax haiku-ish

2. Tanka
Roses are still red
Violets still blue. Although
I still like haiku
I failed to mention sweetness;
so now it is a Tanka.

3. Triolet[6]
Roses are red, so it is said,
but violets are violet,
though we've been told they're blue instead.
Roses are red, so it is said.
Inaccuracies have been spread;
so, this corrective Triolet:
roses, so it is said, are red,
but violets are violet.

---

[6] Before anyone starts hitting up my email, I'm aware that the word, Triolet is pronounced, TREE-o-let, or TREE-o-lay for the truly pretentious among us. But here, we're going to pronounce it TRY-o-let, to rhyme with, VI-o-let. Capiche?

4. Free Verse
Dedicated to Rod McKuen

To be spoken in soft, wistful tones, with soft piano music in the background. (This shit needs all the help it can get.)

the butterfly is drunk on roses and violets.
how many colors of red make up the rose?
how many colors of blue make up the violet?
here alone
on this beach strand
or alone in this crowd
in this Lonesome City
wishing I were not alone
wishing you were here with me
with me on this lonely beach
with me in this lonely crowd

I should have bought you more roses
red roses were your favorite
but now I am blue
as the violet is blue
never again to know
your sugar sweetness

5. A Limerick (that isn't dirty)

There once was a rose that was red
in an old lady's flower bed;
and growing there, too,

were some violets of blue,
or so the prosaism said.

5-a. (An Addendum to the Above)

That cliché line was before us,
so I broke out the old thesaurus.
The last time I heard
that four-syllable word
I fell off my brontosaurus.

6. The Violet Blues
(key of E, boys!)

All them pretty violets, they got the blues.
All them pretty violets, you know they got the blues.
Does that mean them roses all got the Reds?
Sweetie, that's all up to you to choose.

Creation
for Stephen Hawking

*the author has taken a degree of license
with scientific theory...*

...so sue me

A Quark is not the sort of thing
you sort of sit back and enjoy
like a Beatles album or
an "I Love Lucy" marathon
on that retro-classic cable channel.

"Quark" is short for "Quick Spark" and,
so far as I can tell they are
the very tiniest of all
the sub-atomic particles;
three of them will fit inside
an atom's nucleus, and so
if one should land upon your foot
or conk you on the coconut
there isn't any likelihood
that it would leave much of a mark at all.

The only way a Quark is seen
is with one of them new-fangled
particle accelerator
thingies that they got out now
and, dang it, wouldn't you just know,

I've lost the owner's manual to mine.

As far as anyone can tell
the Quark is indivisible
(with liberty and quarkiness
for all), that is, you can't just go
into a greasy spoon and say,
"Hey Doris, I ain't really hungry,
how's about just half a Quark."
But you get your choice of flavor:
you can have the Up, the Down,
the Truth, the Beauty or the Charmed.
(The Charmed are good with mayonnaise.)
You want some coffee with that Quark, or what?

The other thing you ought to know
about that little Quark of ours
is that the Quark does not exist
until it moves, so when it stops
don't bother looking for it anymore.

While our little Quark's out there
it goes about a centimeter
(that is just about the width
of someone's pinky fingernail)
and it meanders on its way
about three-fourths the speed of light;
it's pretty tough to nail one down;
I'm not even sure what color they are.

So, just for fun let's harken back
a couple trillion years or so;
and there's a thing that's kind of like
a Universe except there's nothing
in it but a bunch of Quarks,
some quick and sparky little sparks
of quick and Quarky sparkiness.
There are no bigger sub-atomic
particles to pick on them
or give them Quarky wedgies or to
take their Quarky lunch money away.

There are no planets, moons, or stars,
no "I Love Lucy" marathons,
just sparky, Quarky little sparks
of Quarky little sparky Quarkiness!

> ...and the earth was without form
> and void
> and darkness was upon the face
> of the deep[7]

And God looked out at all the Quarks
buzzing and flitting around in the dark
and snapped His fingers: "I've got an idea!"

And He reached out His mighty arms
and gathered all the Quarks together,

---

[7] Gen 1:2

squoze them all into a bunch
until they were the size of a star,
a planet, a moon, a Ping-Pong ball;
He pushed and squoze till they became
a single geometric point,
then God looked all around and said,

> *"How's about a little light on the subject...."*

About the Author

GABRIEL: Excuse me, Sir. I hate to bother you, but we have a problem with one of the units.

GOD: Oh? What seems to be the trouble?

GABRIEL: Well, Sir, it seems its head was installed upside down.

GOD: Really? Well now whaddya know? Let's have a look...
Ah, sure enough, it's upside down all right.

GABRIEL: Should we just scrap this one, Sir?

GOD: No, no, let's just see if we can make a few minor adjustments.
First, we'll have to flip its nose over so it doesn't drown when it rains.

GABRIEL: That sounds reasonable enough,

GOD: Yes, and as long as it's in the face shop, go ahead and switch the mouth and eyes around. (Don't worry about that... well, you know.)
Then send it on over to ears.

GABRIEL: What about the hair, sir?

GOD: The hair?

GABRIEL: Well, yes Sir, if it's left like this, all of the hair will be on the bottom of its head instead of the top. That might be a little hard to explain.
Should we go ahead and take care of that?

GOD: No, I think the hair department will be tied up all day on that new Justin Bieber model.
Let's just tweak the face a little and toss it onto the seconds pile.
Delaware is always looking for a bargain.

Please Note:

A few of the poems in this volume were originally published in my first book, Fragile Blessings*

To the six people who actually purchased that book, I apologize for the inconvenience.

*Bedford House Publications, 2012
available at https://www.amazon.com/Fragile-Blessings-David-Miller/dp/1479193577

1606-B Ocean Blvd Topsail Beach NC 28445
bedfordhousepub@gmail.com

Made in the USA
Columbia, SC
01 October 2020